The No-Bullying Program

Preventing Bully/Victim Violence at School

Teacher's Manual For Grades 2 & 3

James Bitney—Curriculum Writer

Beverly B. Title, Ph.D.—Program Developer

JOHNSON INSTITUTE®

Minneapolis

Acknowledgment

The contents of this book are based on the No-Bullying Curriculum model originally developed for the St. Vrain Valley School District, Longmont, Colorado, by Beverly B. Title, with assistance from Lisa Anderson-Goebel, Vivian Bray, K.G. Campanella-Green, Ted Goodwin, Karen Greene, Elizabeth Martinson, Mike O'Connell, and Peggy Stortz.

The Bullying Behavior Chart was developed by Beverly B. Title, Ph.D.; Severance Kelly, M.D.; Louis Krupnik, Ph.D.; Joseph Matthews, M.S.W.; Kendra Bartley, M.A.

Curriculum consultation was provided by Peggy O'Connell.

The No-Bullying Program: Preventing Bully/Victim Violence at School

Teacher's Manual for Grades 2 & 3

James Bitney, Curriculum Writer
Beverly B. Title, Ph.D., Program Developer

Copyright ©1996 by Johnson Institute-QVS, Inc. All rights reserved. No part of this manual, except designated student materials and teacher visual aids, may be reproduced or transmitted in any form or by any means, electronic or mechanical, including photocopying or recording, or by any information storage and retrieval system, without express written permission from the publisher.

>Johnson Institute
>7205 Ohms Lane
>Minneapolis, Minnesota 55439-2159
>612-831-1630 or 800-231-5165

ISBN 1-56246-120-6

Logo design: Diana Garcia

Cover and text design: Crombie Design

Artwork by Sally Brewer Lawrence

Printed in the United States of America

96 97 98 99 / 5 4 3 2 1

CONTENTS

Introduction 1
How to Use This Manual 4
    Aims of the program 4
    Learning Strategies 4
        Kinesthetic Learning Tactics 5
        Brainstorming 5
        Drama and Role Playing 6
        Group Discussion 6
        Teaching Masters 6
        Singing 6
    Understanding the Seven- to Eight-year-old Child 7
    Session Components 8

Session 1 10
Session 2 15
Session 3 21
Session 4 26
Session 5 31
Session 6 36

Teaching Masters 40
    Teaching Master 1—No-Bullying Logo Poster 41
    Teaching Master 2—No-Bullying Logos 42
    Teaching Master 3—What's Happening? 43
    Teaching Master 4—Bullying Denny 44
    Teaching Master 5—Feelings List 45
    Teaching Master 6—A Plan for Denny 46
    Teaching Master 7—Tattling or Telling 47
    Teaching Master 8—Bullying Behavior Chart 49
    Teaching Master 9—No More Bullies Song 50

Additional Resources 51
    No-Bullying Program Materials 51
    Video Programs 51
    Publications 52
    Order Form 55

INTRODUCTION
School Zones—Danger Zones

In 1991, 25,000 people were murdered in the United States. During that same year, there were over 67 million handguns in the United States. Sadly, many of the most heavily armed are young people. One official described the arming of America's teenagers as a real "arms race" in which "no one wants to be left behind." Many schools list weapons on campus as one of their top concerns. An eighth grader in a Connecticut junior high school was suspended for refusing to remove his hat. The next day, he came to school with an assault rifle, killed the janitor and wounded the principal and the school secretary.

> A thirteen year old in Florida threatened to torture and kill his social studies teacher after receiving a poor grade on a test. When the boy was arrested, he had two pistols, a box of bullets, and a switchblade.

> After losing a very close foot race, an eighth-grade girl shot the winner, a classmate, in the leg, claiming, "She cheated."

Violence threatens the fiber of our education system both for teachers and for students. In some schools, gun fights have replaced fist fights and "bullet drills" have replaced fire drills. Guns aren't the only weapons at school. Students have been caught with knives, razors, even bombs. Students say they carry weapons for protection. In 1991, over 3 million young people became the victims of violent crime at school.

Teachers do not fare much better than students. A report from the National Education Association indicates that every month of the school year 12% of teachers will have something stolen, 6,000 will have something taken from them forcefully, 120,000 will be threatened, 5,200 will be attacked, and 19% of those attacked will require medical attention.

Violence: A Definition

These startling statistics point out that too many students and teachers are unsafe in their own schools. Too many use violence, witness violence, or are victims of violence. Unfortunately, violence means different things to different people. That is why the Johnson Institute has sought to define violence as:

> **Any word, look, sign, or act that inflicts or threatens to inflict physical or emotional injury or discomfort upon another person's body, feelings, or possessions.**

Violence: A Delineation

Basically, there are two types of violence: peer violence and bully/victim violence.

- Peer violence is defined as acts of violence stemming from disagreements, misunderstandings, or conflicting desires among students who are equally matched in strength and power.

- Bully/victim violence involves an imbalance of power and strength between students; bully/victim violence occurs whenever a student intentionally, repeatedly, and over time inflicts or threatens to inflict physical or emotional injury or discomfort on another's body, feelings, or possessions.

Both kinds must be dealt with to make our schools safe.

Dealing with Bully/Victim Violence: The No-Bullying Program

Schools can successfully deal with the problem of peer violence by helping children grow in social skills: communication, feeling processing, problem solving, conflict management, and conflict mediation. Unfortunately, schools have not been so successful in dealing with bully/victim violence.

The No-Bullying Program has been designed to provide a research-based, educational model to deal with bully/victim violence in the school. Research has clearly shown that bullies do not respond to social skill work. Bullies do not care that what they are doing is creating problems for others. In fact, they generally enjoy the results of their bullying behavior. The *No-Bullying Program* offers schools a plan for dealing with bullies and bully/victim violence.

Approximately 15% of any school population are bullies or victims of bullies, which means that 85% of the school population are relatively uninvolved in bullying behaviors. To end bullying, the *No-Bullying Program* engages the help of that 85% by:

- Clearly defining what is and what is not bullying
- Creating empathy for the victims of bullying
- Teaching students when and how to report bullying
- Establishing clear consequences for bullying that are strictly enforced by everyone in the school

To assure the help of that 85%, the *No-Bullying Program* also insists that *all adults* in the school take more proactive roles in dealing with bullies and their victims. Research has shown that adult intervention is crucial to ending bully/victim violence. Once children realize that reporting bullying to an adult will result in immediate intervention and action (consequences), they feel secure in becoming proactive in ending bullying themselves.

Prior to meeting with the children, you have met with all school staff and support staff to:

- overview the *No-Bullying Program* in its entirety; review research and correct misinformation about bullying: its perpetrators and its victims
- learn how to stop enabling bullying behavior
- agree on a school-wide policy of no-entitlement and no-tolerance with regard to bullying behaviors
- learn intervention strategies with regard to bullying behaviors
- create support networks with community leaders and service providers, professionals in the areas of violence and domestic abuse, law enforcement officials, student leaders, and parent advisory group leaders or members
- establish a procedure enabling the children to feel safe when reporting bullying
- set, and commit to the consistent enforcement of, school-wide consequences for bullying behaviors

Now, as a teacher, your role in the project is to lead the children through an exciting educational process designed to empower them to end bullying in their school and to make it "Safe Zone" for learning.

How to Use This Manual

This *Teacher's Manual* offers you material and detailed guidance to lead second and third graders through six 30- to 40-minute sessions of interactive learning. You may lengthen or shorten the session time, depending on the deletion or addition of an activity and your particular teaching style.

Aims of the Program

To teach strategically formulated awarenesses and skills that are designed to help the children:

- understand the *No-Bullying Program*
- define bullying, disclose personal experiences with bully/victim problems, and heighten their awareness of these problems
- define and enumerate bullying behaviors
- develop empathy for the victims of bullying
- recognize the distinction between tattling and telling in order to get help in a bullying situation
- learn the school-wide consequences for engaging in bullying behaviors

Learning Strategies

The *No-Bullying Program* incorporates a variety of strategies to help you facilitate learning. These strategies include:

- Kinesthetic learning tactics
- Brainstorming
- Drama and role playing

- Group discussion
- Teaching Masters
- Singing

Kinesthetic Learning Tactics

An ancient Oriental proverb states: "Tell me, I'll forget. Show me, I may remember. But involve me, and I'll understand." Put simply, kinesthetic learning techniques *involve* the children. Using these techniques allows you to appeal to more than one sense of the learner. They even allow you to get learners moving, so that body muscles may respond to the learning stimuli.

When the children hear you say something and, at the same time, see some information you've printed on the board or newsprint, they retain more of what you're saying. As you teach, then, frequently write out words and terms as you say them. Likewise, capture attention by using sight as well as hearing. If you write a word or term, circle, star, box, underline, or check it if you refer to it a second or third time. Draw lines and arrows to connect words—to draw connections between terms. Consider using different colored chalk or markers to show relationships or connections between words and terms. This does more than add color; it makes relationships stand out.

Avail yourself of every opportunity to get the children on their feet, writing or underlining items on the board or newsprint, raising their hands, and moving about the room. Encourage them to use all their senses as they learn.

Brainstorming

Brainstorming allows everyone to speak quickly and briefly and puts the burden of knowledge on no one person. Brainstorming is proof of the adage that "All of us are smarter than any one of us." Brainstorming is an activity that's easy to do and with which almost all children are comfortable, since every brainstorming response or idea is an acceptable one.

When the children brainstorm, list their responses (or words that describe them) on the board or newsprint, but don't add your comments, for example: "Good!" "Just what I was thinking." "I don't see how that fits, but I'll write it down anyway." "Do you really mean that?" Your comments, either positive or negative, can prevent some children from saying anything at all or can embarrass others. Be aware that as the children brainstorm, a type of cooperation takes place. Initial responses elicit new responses that pull together many ideas into one. This synergism tends to energize the children and make them eager to join in.

When brainstorming, be wary of searching for "the right response" and then stopping the brainstorming once somebody gives it. Instead, set a time limit for brainstorming and get all the responses you can during that time. Or simply end the brainstorming when the children stop coming up with ideas.

Finally, brainstorming helps children realize that they already know a great deal, that the answers to questions they may have already lie within them. Thus brainstorming helps the children value themselves and appreciate that you value them.

Drama and Role Playing

In drama (skits) and role playing, children assume various characters and create roles. During role play, they may explore situations, identify problems, resolve conflicts, and create solutions. In other words, they deal with real-life matters in a safe situation. They can experience a whole range of emotions as they identify with characters and roles and work toward creative solutions. These activities can provide insights for the children that simple discussion cannot.

At the conclusion of a drama (skit) or role play, always offer those who took part the opportunity to express and process their feelings. Likewise, offer the observers the chance to share their observations and perceptions.

Group Discussion

In group discussion a synergy that is more than just the sum of the number of children in the group can result from their talking together and sharing ideas. The sum becomes more than the addition of its parts.

Teaching Masters

This level of the *No-Bullying Program* provides you with 8 Teaching Masters (see pages 41–50), which you can reproduce as handouts for the children. The children use them as worksheets to explore the key concepts of a particular session.

Singing

This level of *The No-Bullying Program* uses singing within the Concluding Activity of each session. It does so, first of all, because children love singing. Moreover, singing also adds a spirit of celebration, joy, and excitement to learning. At this age, the children learn to sing by listening and repeating a song line by line (rote singing). If you sing a song through and then repeat it phrase by phrase and have the children sing it after you, they will be able to sing the complete song. The song used in this level of *The No-Bullying Program* is set to a well-known melody. Words and musical notation for the song can be found on page 50, as well as in each session.

> **Note:** If you do not consider yourself a singer and/or are uncomfortable singing, ask someone to make you a tape recording that you can use with the children.

Understanding the Seven- to Eight-year-old Child

For the most part, the following characteristics—all of which are *normal*—are exhibited by the seven- to eight-year-old child. He or she:

- trusts adults and older children

- seeks adult encouragement and reassurance and is dependent on parents for support, direction, and approval

- is very sensitive to both praise and criticism

- knows right from wrong, but only by being told so by adults

- is often unsure of how he or she is behaving (e.g., evidence questions like, "Am I being good?")

- is interested in the work, concerns, and opinions of parents and other trusted adults

- learns in the concrete; that is, by doing; needs and enjoys hands-on learning and repetition

- has a clear sex identity and prefers to be with his or her own sex

- has a brief attention span; needs a variety of activities to stimulate interest

- requires a stable, consistent environment for learning

- possesses a rich dream and fantasy life and likes to explore them as much as the real world

- is often moved by images and fantasies, but can also be terrified by frightening or destructive images

- is often inconsistent in behavior

- possesses a sense of justice and fairness based on reciprocity ("If I do good, I will be rewarded. If I do bad, I will be punished.")

- is often not aware of the perspective or feelings of others

- exhibits shyness around unfamiliar people

- can feel jealousy toward siblings and friends

- has occasional outbursts of temper and inappropriate behavior

- is not always able to identify, own, and express feelings suitably or appropriately

Session Components

- **Aim** states the overall goal of the session.

- **Objectives** lists the learning outcomes of the session.

- **Materials** catalogues all the teaching devices necessary to present the session.

- **Preparing for the Session** contains directions for all the pre-session arrangements necessary to present the session.

- **Background for the Teacher** includes pertinent information:

    — to help you set the educational content in context

    — to provide you with added information for personal growth

    — to give you new data necessary to present the session with the greatest success.

- **Session Plan** includes the specific steps or directions for presenting the session. Each **Session Plan** is composed of three parts: *Beginning the Session, Leading the Session,* and *Concluding the Session.*

    — *Beginning the Session* serves to welcome and gather the children, unite them as a group, review previous learning, and get them ready to work and share together.

    — *Leading the Session* includes learning activities, discussions, exercises, drama or role play, as well as other educational processes, presented in a clear, step-by-step design that enables you to guide the children through the session.

— *Concluding the Session*, which remains relatively the same for every session, includes activities that serve to affirm the children in what they learned during the session and to help them commit themselves to No-bullying both as individuals and as a school community.

Finally, some of the plans include an Optional Activity, which you may choose to use to replace an activity in the plan, to enhance the plan, or to extend the session.

This session plan format strives to give the children a total experience that is structured but hospitable, instructive but creative, and challenging but supportive. Because the format remains constant for each session, it also meets the needs of at-risk children for structure, stability, consistency, and enjoyment. You may use the plans with confidence.

Session 1

Aim

To introduce the *No-Bullying Program* to the children

Objectives

By the end of the session, the children will

- recognize and understand the No-Bullying logo
- begin to identify bullying and its effects
- appreciate that their school is committed to ending bullying

Materials

- copy of the No-Bullying logo poster (Teaching Master 1)
- newsprint and marker
- cut-outs of the No-Bullying logos (Teaching Master 2)
- posterboard backing cut-outs
- colored markers or crayons, glue sticks or paste
- safety pins and tape
- optional: *The Hundred Dresses* by Eleanor Estes (see page 52)

Preparing for the Session

Carefully read over the session plan in advance. Make a copy of the No-Bullying logo poster (Teaching Master 1) to be used throughout the sessions. Make copies of the No-Bullying logos (Teaching Master 2), enough so that each child can have his or her own logo, with which he or she will fashion a badge. Pre-cut the logos from the sheets. Using one of the logos as a guide, from posterboard, cut out backing for each of the logos. Have safety pins available, one for each child.

> **Note:** If your school is so equipped, you might consider simply laminating the badges, thus eliminating the need for posterboard backing and safety pins.

Review the song, "No More Bullies," which is sung to the tune of "Sailing, Sailing," and will be used to conclude each session. Although the words and music for "No More Bullies" are contained in each session, a larger version of the words and music may also be found on page 50 of this manual.

Finally, if you choose to use the Optional Activity, make all necessary arrangements and adjustments to the Session Plan.

Background for the Teacher

It is important for you, as a teacher, to understand that bullying is not always obvious. It most often takes place in concealed areas. At school, bullying occurs where you're not present or where you can't see: in bathrooms, in hallways, on playground areas that are difficult to supervise, in empty classrooms, etc. Simply because you do not witness bullying behaviors does not mean they aren't taking place.

Session Plan

Beginning the Session

Gather the children in a circle. Join the circle yourself. Introduce yourself and offer your own words of welcome. Then, beginning with the child on your right, go around the circle, having each child introduce himself or herself and then tell one thing that makes him or her feel safe at school.

Leading the Session

1. Display the copy of the No-Bullying logo poster. Ask the children what they think it may mean. Accept all replies and list them on a sheet of newsprint.

2. Drawing on the children's ideas, lead a discussion about the logo with the group. Encourage the children to share:

   - what types of things they think bullying children do

- what happens to children who bully others
- what happens to children who are being bullied
- how bullying affects their school.

Again, as you discuss, list children's ideas on newsprint.

Note: Save the newsprint sheet for use in Step 4 below, and again in Session 2.

3. After the discussion, tell the children that they will be talking more about bullying behavior—about children taking unfair advantage of others—for the next few weeks. Point out that your school wants to help stop all bullying and getting hurt by bullying in your school. Then say:

   "In our class time together, we will learn how to help each other and how and when to tell a trusted adult about bullying. However, whenever we talk about bullying *in this class*, we will never call anyone by name who is bullying or being bullied."

To reinforce the importance of this boundary issue, teach the children the following rhyme.

In our class time together,
no bullying's our aim.
But we'll never charge a classmate
with bullying by name.

If you wish, write the rhyme on the board or newsprint. Go through the rhyme with the children until they know it by heart. Likewise, add movement to the rhyme.

4. Drawing on their ideas from the discussion in Step 2, help the children express:

- why they think bullies do what they do.
- how they think a bully may feel.
- how they think being bullied might make them feel.

Add the children's ideas to the sheet begun in Step 2.

As the children get into talking about feelings, help them to avoid calling feelings "good" or "bad." Instead, encourage them to *name* feelings more specifically; for example, "sad," "angry," "frightened," "ashamed," etc. If the children have difficulty in naming feelings, invite them to show the feeling on their faces or with their bodies.

Tell the children that you will save the newsprint sheet with their ideas for the next time they meet. Say:

> "In our next session, we will identify bullying behavior and we'll see if we need to make changes on this sheet."

5. Tell the children that they will make their own No-Bullying badges to wear. Distribute cut-outs of the No-Bullying logo and crayons or colored markers. Invite the children to choose any color they wish and to color the logo's circle and slash mark. Then pass out the posterboard backing cut-outs you prepared prior to the session and the glue sticks or paste. Direct the children to affix their colored logos to the posterboard backing. Finally, have the children use tape to attach a safety pin to the back of their badges. Some of the children may need help pinning on their badges, so, as the children work, circulate and offer help where needed. (Note: Or, as mentioned in Preparing for the Session above, laminate the badges for the children.)

6. When the children finish, compliment them on their work. Encourage them to wear their No-Bullying badges at school. Tell the group that everyone in your school will be working hard at stopping all bullying in school. Once again, assure the children that they will be learning ways to help one another and learning how and when to tell a trusted adult about bullying.

7. Teach the children the song, "No More Bullies." It is sung to the tune of "Sailing, Sailing." If you wish, make copies of the words for the children or have the words written on a large sheet of newsprint.

Concluding the Session

Have the children form a circle around you. Direct them to place their arms around one another's shoulders. Set the copy of the No-Bullying logo poster on the floor in the center of the circle. Join the circle yourself. Invite the children to sing "No More Bullies:"

Ask the children to show that they "stand together" in ending bullying in their school by taking one small step forward, thus tightening the circle.

If you wish, conclude with handshakes or high-fives all around.

Collect any extraneous materials. Remind the children of the time of their next session when they will identify bullying behavior.

Optional Activity

After Step 2, read *The Hundred Dresses* by Eleanor Estes to the children. It is a wonderful tale about what bullying is and can do. Note, however, that sharing the story will easily double the time allotted for the session. Therefore, if you choose to use the book, plan on extending this initial session over two meeting times.

SESSION 2

Aim

To help the children define bullying, disclose experiences with bully/victim problems, and heighten their awareness of these problems.

Objectives

By the end of the session, the children will

- define bullying
- share experience of—and become more aware of—bullying and its effects
- better understand that their school is committed to ending bullying

Materials

- copy of the No-Bullying logo poster
- chalkboard and chalk or newsprint and marker
- newsprint sheet from Session 1
- posterboard
- copies of the survey, "What's Happening?" (Teaching Master 3)
- pencils

Preparing for the Session

Carefully read through the session plan in advance. With a marker or art letters, on a piece of posterboard, make a poster that reads:

> **BULLYING HAPPENS...**
>
> when someone with *greater* power
>
> *unfairly* hurts someone
>
> with *less* power
>
> *over and over again.*

Note: You will need this poster in this session and again in Session 3. Make copies of the survey "What's Happening?" (Teaching Master 3) so that each child has his or her own copy. Make sure that the copy of the No-Bullying logo poster is prominently displayed in the meeting space.

Background for the Teacher

Besides using the survey, "What's Happening?" during this session, feel free to re-use it at any time you feel the need to do a perception check on bullying. Whenever you administer the survey, be sure to share results with other school staff. That way, your school will have a broader perspective on the problem.

Session Plan

Beginning the Session

Gather the children in a circle. Draw attention to the copy of the No-Bullying logo poster. Invite volunteers to recall what the logo means. To remind the children that whenever they talk about bullying in class they should not call by name anyone who may be bullying or being bullied, lead them in the following rhyme, which they learned in Session 1:

> *In our class time together,*
> *no bullying's our aim.*
> *But we'll never charge a classmate*
> *with bullying by name.*

Leading the Session

1. To introduce this session, display the newsprint sheet of the children's ideas, which you saved from Session 1. Briefly go through the material on the sheet, reminding the children of what they thought were:

   - the types of things bullying children do
   - what happens to children who bully others
   - what happens to children who are being bullied
   - how bullying affects their school.

2. Display the "Bullying Happens" poster you prepared prior to the session and read it aloud to the group.

> BULLYING HAPPENS...
>
> **when someone with *greater* power**
>
> *unfairly* **hurts someone**
>
> **with *less* power**
>
> *over and over again.*

Then divide the board or newsprint into three columns, labeling them as follows:

Physical Strength **Verbal Ability** **Social Skills**

Explain these concepts to the students, giving examples of each one. Tell the group that if someone has greater "power" than someone else in any of these three areas and uses that "power" to hurt over and over, that is bullying.

Once again, draw attention to the newsprint sheet of children's ideas, which you saved from Session 1 and used in Step 1 above. Drawing on the behaviors the children thought of, have them determine what sort of "power" is being used and then list it under the appropriate heading on the board or newsprint. For example:

Physical Strength	Verbal Ability	Social Skills
size	threats	humiliating
hitting	insults	excluding
pushing	name calling	hurting feelings
stealing	teasing	playing mean trick
defacing/destroying property	making fun of another	

Stress that bullying happens whenever someone *unfairly* uses power to hurt someone else over and over again.

3. Tell the children that now that they have a definition of bullying, they will be completing an important survey about bullying. Make sure the children understand that the survey is not a test. Explain that the survey simply asks them to respond to statements about their life at school. Point out that there are no right or wrong answers and that some of the items may have more than one answer. Tell the children that as they respond to each statement, they should mark as many answers as apply to them.

4. Distribute pencils and copies of the survey, "What's Happening?" (Teaching Master 3) and direct the children to complete it. If, however, you feel that the children would be better served by your reading the statements and possible responses aloud, simply go through the survey with the children.

5. When everyone is finished, help the children better "own" the survey by drawing attention to statement #4 *(I think that most of the bullying that happens at our school happens…)*. Then, ask the children to raise their hands if they checked the first possible response *(in classrooms)*. Have one of the children record the number of responses on the board or newsprint. Go on to do the same for the five remaining possible responses. Finally, have the children count up the responses and determine what they, as a group, believe to be the place(s) in their school where most bullying happens.

6. Go on to repeat the above procedure for statement #9 *(To help me feel safe at school, I think adults should…)*. Ask a different child to act as recorder.

Afterward, assure the children that you will convey their concerns about where bullying takes place in their school, what they'd like adults to do about it, as well as all other information from their surveys to other adults in the school, including the principal.

Collect the pencils and surveys.

Concluding the Session

Have the children form a circle around you. Direct them to place their arms around one another's shoulders. Set the copy of the No-Bullying logo poster on the floor in the center of the circle. Remind the children of the definition of bullying:

BULLYING HAPPENS…

when someone with *greater* power

unfairly hurts someone

with *less* power

over and over again.

Then join the circle yourself and lead the children in singing the "No More Bullies" song:

No more bul-lies! That is our gol-den rule. All of us stand to end all bul-ly-ing that's in our school. No more bul-lies, hurt-ing or caus-ing fear. All of us pledge to work un-til there's no more bul-lies here.

Ask the children to show that they "stand together" and support one another in ending bullying in their school by taking two small steps forward, tightening the circle.

If you wish, conclude with handshakes or high-fives all around.

Remind the children of the time of their next session. Tell them that when they meet, they will look at some examples of bullying and how it affects others.

Session 3

Aim

To help the children define and enumerate bullying behaviors

Objectives

By the end of the session, the children will

- identify and create a list of bullying behaviors
- better appreciate how being bullied feels

Materials

- copy of the No-Bullying logo poster
- "Bullying Happens" poster from Session 2
- copy of the Bullying Behavior chart (see page 49) [For teacher use only.]
- newsprint and markers and tape
- copies of "Bullying Denny" (Teaching Master 4)
- lined writing paper and pencils
- optional: *The Rag Coat* by Lauren A. Mills (see page 53)

Preparing for the Session

Carefully read through the session plan. Decide on five children to take part in "Bullying Denny," a skit about bullying behaviors (Teaching Master 4). Four children will play children who bully; one will play their victim (Denny). Note:

Take care not to select a victim or perpetrator of bullying to play the role of Denny. Likewise, during the session, be cautious not to identify or imply by name any students who engage in bullying behaviors or who are victims of such behavior. Make six copies of "Bullying Denny" (Teaching Master 4), one for each participant in the skit, and one for yourself. Make a "Bullying Behaviors" poster by dividing a large sheet of newsprint into three columns as below:

Bullying Behaviors

| Hurting someone's body or things | Hurting someone's feelings | Hurting someone's friendships |

Make a copy of the Bullying Behavior chart (see page 49). Review the chart prior to the session and have it handy for your own use as you lead the children through Step 7 in the session plan. Consider using the Optional Activity, being sure to make necessary arrangements. See to it that the No-Bullying logo poster is displayed prominently in the meeting space.

Background for the Teacher

Studies have shown that bullying behaviors include not only forms of physical aggression, but also emotional harassment, social alienation, and both subtle and overt intimidation (the latter often being—but not exclusively—the behavior of girls who engage in bullying). No matter the type, bullying behaviors are usually difficult to detect. However, as a teacher, you need to be aware that all types of bullying occur at school. Likewise, it's also important to remember that bullying behaviors are *learned*. As such, they can be unlearned.

Session Plan

Beginning the Session

Gather the children in a circle. Draw attention to the copy of the No-Bullying logo poster. Ask the children to recall some of the things they talked about that bullies do. Ask:

- What types of things do bullies do that make them different from other kids? *(Look for responses that evidence the children's understanding that bullying stems from a position of power and is repetitive.)*

Go on to invite the group to recall the survey from Session 2. Then ask:

- How does bullying affect our school?

Leading the Session

1. Display the "Bullying Happens" poster from Session 2. Ask a volunteer to read it aloud.

> BULLYING HAPPENS...
>
> when someone with *greater* power
>
> *unfairly* hurts someone
>
> with *less* power
>
> *over and over again.*

Consider leaving the "Bullying Happens" poster displayed in the room for the remainder of the sessions.

2. Distribute lined writing paper and pencils. Write the following on the board or newsprint: "I think some kids bully other kids because…" Read the statement aloud and have the children copy it onto their papers. Tell the children to think about the statement and then to write at least two reasons why they think some kids bully others.

3. While the group is working, silently take aside the five children you decided upon prior to the session to be in the skit. Give each child a copy of "Bullying Denny" and assign roles. Explain to the children that they will be doing a skit for the group. Tell the children acting as "bullies" that they are to pretend to be following "Denny" around the playground harassing him, but to remember they are just pretending, for they cannot hurt "Denny." Tell "Denny" that he is not to react by fighting back or saying anything mean to the other actors. Instead, the child playing "Denny" should simply *show* with his or her face and/or body how he or she thinks "Denny" would feel. Allow the children a few moments to practice.

4. While the "actors" are practicing, invite the rest of the children to share what they wrote in response to the question, "Why do you think some kids bully other kids?" After everyone who desires has had a chance to respond, tell the children that they are now going to view a skit put on by

some of their classmates that will help them learn more about bullying behaviors—about what bullies do.

5. Invite the "actors" to present their skit for the group. Afterward, thank the children and have them take their places with the group.

6. Lead the children in a discussion about the skit. Begin by asking the child who played Denny how it felt being the victim of bullying. Then, go on to ask the group:

   - If you were Denny, how would you feel?
   - Why would you feel that way?
   - Why would the other kids gang up on Denny?
   - Do you think it's okay for the other kids to say and do what they said and did to Denny?

   Be sure the children recognize how being the victim of bullying would make them feel.

7. Display the "Bullying Behaviors" poster you made prior to the session.

Bullying Behaviors

Hurting someone's body or things	Hurting someone's feelings	Hurting someone's friendships

Invite the children to name and discuss the behaviors displayed by the children who were bullying during the skit. List these behaviors under the appropriate columns on the poster.

Note: As the children offer their suggestions, use the Bullying Behavior Chart as a referent to suggest behaviors that could be added to their list.

Draw attention to the "Bullying Happens" poster to emphasize that the listed behaviors are bullying *only when they are used **repeatedly** by someone with **greater power** over someone with **less power**.*

Afterward, tell the children that you will keep the "Bullying Behaviors" poster displayed in the room and that you will continue to use this list (and add to it if necessary) to help them better recognize and deal with the problem of bullying in their school.

Concluding the Session

Have the children form a circle around you. Direct them to place their arms around one another's shoulders. Set the copy of the No-Bullying logo poster on the floor in the center of the circle. Join the circle yourself. Then lead the children in singing "No More Bullies:"

Ask the children to show that they "stand together" and support one another in ending bullying in their school by taking three small steps forward, tightening the circle.

If you wish, conclude with handshakes or high-fives all around.

Remind the children of the time of their next session. Tell them that they will be learning a lot more about children who are victims of bullying.

Optional Activity

Instead of presenting the skit, "Bullying Denny," you may substitute a reading of the story, *The Rag Coat* by Lauren A. Mills. After the reading, simply adapt the questions in Step 6 and the directions in Step 7 to the story. Note, however, that sharing the story will lengthen the session. You may need to extend it over two meeting times.

Session 4

Aim

To help the children develop empathy for the victims of bullying

Objectives

By the end of the session, the children will

- increase their level of empathy for those victimized by bullying

Materials

- copy of the No-Bullying logo poster
- "Bullying Behaviors" poster from Session 3
- copies of "Feelings List" (Teaching Master 5)
- newsprint and markers and tape
- drawing paper and crayons or colored markers
- butcher paper
- tape
- copies of "A Plan for Denny" (Teaching Master 6)

Preparing for the Session

Carefully read through the session plan in advance. Use a long sheet of butcher paper to make a banner. In large letters, write the phrase "Bullying Makes Us Feel…" Make copies of "Feelings List" (Teaching Master 5) and "A Plan for Denny" (Teaching Master 6), one of each for each child. Review the story in

Step 3; decide on the best way to present it to the children. Be sure that the No-Bullying logo poster and the "Bullying Behaviors" poster are displayed prominently in the room.

Background for the Teacher

No one deserves to be bullied. Bullying can occur only when a person with greater power takes advantage of someone with less power. Children who are victims of bullying devote great energy to avoid being bullied. Nearly all their activity at school is focused on getting and staying safe. To end bullying and to help its victims, *all* the children need to learn to understand and empathize with them. Too often, however, such empathy is channeled into aggression against the person who is exhibiting the bullying behavior. Unfortunately, this does little to end bullying. Children who bully are excited by victims who fight back and by aggression from others who "take the victim's side." As you lead the children through this session, take care not to allow the children's empathy for the victims of bullying to turn to aggression against those who are bullying. The goal is not to avenge victims of bullying, but to help them feel protected and safe at school.

Session Plan

Beginning the Session

Gather the children in a circle. Point out the "Bullying Behaviors" poster they made during their last session. Ask if anyone would like to add to it. Afterward, remind the children that you will keep the poster displayed in the room and that you will continue to use it to help them deal with the problem of bullying in their school.

Leading the Session

1. Display the No-Bullying logo poster. Distribute copies of the "Feelings List" (Teaching Master 5). Tell the children that they can use the names of the feelings on the list to help them tell how children their age might feel in different situations. Ask the children the questions listed below, each of which begins:

"How might someone your age feel if he or she…"

- just made the winning score in a game?

- ate a whole box of chocolate candy?

- won a prize?

- lost a favorite toy?

- had an argument with a best friend?

- got called on in class and didn't know the answer?

Go on to ask:

"What types of things might make someone your age feel…"

- happy?

- sad?

- lonely?

- nervous?

- afraid?

2. Invite the children to recall the skit about Denny from their last session. Ask volunteers to explain what happened to Denny. Encourage the children to draw from their copies of the "Feelings List" to tell (or show with their faces or bodies) how they think Denny felt.

3. Have the children quiet themselves inside and outside to hear a story. Explain that the story comes from a diary written by someone their age. (**Note:** if necessary, tell the children what a diary is.) Then, either read the following story to the children or, better, tell it in your own words.

> Dear Diary,
>
> I hate school! I wish I didn't have to go. Some of the kids there are always picking on me. They're mean. They follow me around the playground. They make fun of me. They always say they're going to beat me up. It's not fair! I'm scared all the time.
>
> One day, this really big kid pushed me down and took my lunch. I didn't know what to do, so I just went hungry. Last week, this girl colored all over a picture I drew. I handed it in, but it was a mess. The teacher told me that I was not a good worker. See, even the teacher doesn't like me.

I want to punch those kids who are bullying me and tell them to leave me alone or go away, but I just can't. I get this real sick feeling in my stomach. It makes me want to cry, but I know that would just make them laugh.

Even the kids that used to be my friends aren't anymore. Maybe they're afraid of getting hurt, too. Or maybe they just don't like me anymore. I don't know. What I do know is that I wish some big giant would come in the middle of the night and squish the school. Then I wouldn't have to go there.

What do you think, Diary? What should I do? Do you have a plan? I don't.

Your friend,

Denny

4. Invite the children to share their initial reactions to the story. Then draw attention to their copies of the "Feelings List" and ask:

   - How does Denny feel?

   - Do you think Denny has a right to feel the way he does?

   - How do you feel when you see someone else being bullied?

5. Distribute drawing paper and crayons or colored markers. Divide the children into two groups. Have the children in the first group draw a picture that shows how someone their age might feel if *he or she* were being bullied. Have the children in the second group draw a picture that shows how someone their age might feel if he or she saw *someone else* being bullied.

   While the children draw, post the banner "Bullying Makes Us Feel," which you prepared prior to the session. When the children finish, call on members of the first group to explain their drawings to the class. Then invite all in the first group to tape their drawings under the banner. Go on to call on members of the second group to explain their drawings to the class. Then invite all in the second group to tape their drawings under the banner. Point out that bullying never makes people feel happy.

6. Re-read the last paragraph of the story to the children. Then ask:

   - What could you do if you were being bullied or you saw someone else being bullied?

   Accept all replies, but gently discourage any suggestions of retaliation.

7. Distribute pencils and copies of "A Plan for Denny" (Teaching Master 6). Go through the steps outlined on the sheet *with* the children. Point out that no one deserves to be bullied, but that bullying back is not a good plan. Stress the importance of telling a caring adult about the bullying. Explain to the children that at their next session they will learn more about the need to tell a caring adult about bullying and how to do it. Emphasize that the adults in your school *do* care and *will* step in to help stop bullying.

Collect crayons or markers and pencils.

Concluding the Session

Have the children form a circle around you. Direct them to place their arms around one another's shoulders. Place the copy of the No-Bullying logo poster on the floor in the center of the circle. Join the circle yourself. Then lead the children in singing "No More Bullies":

No More Bullies Song

No more bul - lies! That is our gol - den rule.
All of us stand to end all bul - ly - ing that's in our school. No more bul - lies, hurt - ing or caus - ing fear. All of us pledge to work un - til there's no more bul - lies here.

Ask the children to show that they "stand together" and support one another in ending bullying in their school by taking four small steps forward, tightening the circle.

If you wish, conclude with handshakes or high-fives all around. Remind the children of their next meeting time. Tell them that they will discover something very important about how to get help in a bullying situation.

Session 5

Aim

To help the children recognize the distinction between tattling and telling in order to get help in a bullying situation

Objectives

By the end of the session, the children will

- define both tattling and telling
- understand the difference between tattling and telling
- recognize that they need to tell someone they trust about bullying to get help
- appreciate how adults in their school are willing to help stop bullying
- learn their school's procedure for reporting bullying behavior

Materials

- copy of the No-Bullying logo poster
- "Bullying Behaviors" poster from Session 3
- chalkboard and chalk or newsprint and marker
- posterboard
- copies of "Tattling or Telling?" (Teaching Master 7)
- pencils

Preparing for the Session

Carefully read through the entire session plan prior to presenting the session. With a marker or art letters, on a piece of posterboard, make a poster that reads:

> **Tattling is talking to someone about a problem just to get someone else in trouble, to get my own way, or to make myself look good.**

On a second sheet of posterboard, make another poster that reads:

> **Telling is talking to someone I trust about a problem because I or someone else may be getting hurt.**

Make each child a copy of "Tattling or Telling?" (Teaching Master 7). Be ready to explain to the children the procedure your school has previously agreed upon for reporting bullying.

Carefully consider using this sessions two Optional Activities. See to it that the No-Bullying logo poster and the "Bullying Behaviors" poster are displayed prominently in the meeting space.

Background for the Teacher

Although second and third graders are beginning to develop a sense of fairness—at least as far as self is concerned—they resist turning on one another. This is not to say that normal seven and eight year olds don't tattle on one another, for indeed they do. However, they generally do so to get their own way or to look "better" in the eyes of adults. Your challenge in presenting this session is to help the children recognize that it is appropriate to "tell" when they are being bullied or when they witness bullying, while discouraging tattling. An open and nonjudgmental attitude on your part will go a long way in helping children "tell," not "tattle."

Remember, children who are victims of bullying are afraid to tell. They fear both physical retribution and social ostracism. Make sure that the children understand that you and all school staff are committed to protecting the victims of bullying and that children reported for bullying will be watched by you and others at your school and will be held responsible for any further bullying behavior.

Session Plan

Beginning the Session

Gather the children in a circle. Draw attention to the copy of the No-Bullying logo poster. Invite the children to recall the story about Denny and his diary that they heard in their last session. Then ask what they think would be the best thing to do if:

- they were being bullied
- they saw someone else being bullied

Conclude by telling the children that in this session they will learn how to *tell* about bullying and get help without feeling that they're *tattling*.

Leading the Session

1. Write the word "Tattling" on the board or newsprint. Ask the children to brainstorm what they think tattling is. Record all ideas on the board or newsprint.

2. Drawing on the children's ideas, help them recognize that tattling is talking to someone about a problem:

   - just to get someone else in trouble
   - just to get their own way
   - just to make themselves look good and someone else look bad

   Tell the children when we do these things, we're tattling.

3. Display the definition of tattling on the "Tattling" poster you made prior to the session. Read the definition aloud to the group:

   Tattling is speaking to someone about a problem just to get someone else in trouble, to get my own way, or to make myself look good.

   Invite the children to offer examples of tattling. If the children confuse "tattling" with "telling," gently correct the misunderstanding.

4. Write the word "Telling" on the board or newsprint. Ask the children to brainstorm what they think telling is. Record all ideas on the board or newsprint.

5. Drawing on the children's ideas, help them recognize that telling is speaking to an adult about a problem in order to get help for oneself or another. Then go on to display the definition of telling on the "Telling" poster you made prior to the session. Read the definition aloud to the group:

   Telling is speaking to someone I trust about a problem because I or someone else may be getting hurt.

   Invite the children to offer examples of telling. Again, should the children confuse "telling" with "tattling," gently correct the misunderstanding.

6. Distribute pencils and copies of "Tattling or Telling?" (Teaching Master 7). Read each of the four stories with the group. (**Note:** Depending on the reading level of the children, you may ask volunteers to read the stories.) After reading the first story, read the follow-up question aloud and have the children circle whether they think the child in the story was "tattling" or "telling." Do the same for each of the remaining three stories. Afterward, go back over each story, asking for a show of hands to determine who circled "tattling" and who circled "telling" for each story. (Note: The correct responses are: "Missy" = tattling; "Luiz" = telling; "Shanna" = telling; "Jamhal" = tattling.)

7. Take time to discuss the difference between tattling and telling. In the discussion, help the children understand that tattling gets someone *into* trouble, while telling helps get someone *out of* trouble. Emphasize to the children that when they are being bullied and hurt on the inside or outside, or when they see someone else being bullied and hurt that way, **they need to *tell* a trusted adult in their school.**

   Outline for the children the procedure your school has previously agreed upon for reporting bullying (e.g., *how* they are to report, *to whom* they are to report, *when and where* they are to report, etc.). Make sure the children understand that when they "tell" about bullying, their anonymity will be insured, re-emphasizing that an adult *will* step in to help and protect.

Collect pencils.

Concluding the Session

Have the children form a circle around you. Direct them to place their arms around one another's shoulders. Set the copy of the No-Bullying logo poster on the floor in the center of the circle. Join the circle yourself. Then lead the children in singing "No More Bullies:"

No More Bullies Song

No more bullies! That is our golden rule.
All of us stand to end all bullying that's in our school. No more
bullies, hurting or causing fear. All of us pledge to
work until there's no more bullies here.

Ask the children to show that they "stand together" and support one another in ending bullying in their school by taking five small steps forward, tightening the circle.

If you wish, conclude with handshakes or high-fives all around.

Remind the children of their next meeting time. Tell them that when next they meet, the principal will join them to explain what will happen to children who are bullying.

Optional Activities

1. To extend the session, divide the class into small groups and have them role play "telling" adults to get help. This will give the children needed practice and confidence in approaching adults for aid. It will also help them better distinguish between tattling and telling.

    You may want to invite older students (from the fourth and/or fifth grades) or peer counselors or conflict mediators to present a few role plays to the children in your class in order to give them appropriate examples of "telling" to get help.

2. To enhance Step 7, create a "Bullying Report Card" to give each child to serve as a reminder of your school's procedure for reporting bullying. Simply outline the procedure and have it duplicated on index cards or easy-to-carry sheets that the children can keep with them.

Session 6

Aim

To present school-wide consequences for engaging in bullying behaviors

Objectives

By the end of the session, the children will

- understand the meaning of consequences
- know the school-wide consequences for bullying
- better understand that all adults in the school are committed to making the school a safe and secure place

Materials

- copy of the No-Bullying logo poster
- "Bullying Behaviors" poster from Session 3
- chalkboard and chalk or newsprint and marker
- posterboard or newsprint and markers
- tape

Preparing for the Session

Carefully read through the session plan in advance. Prior to the session, use posterboard or newsprint to make a large poster entitled "Bullying Consequences." With the aid and consensus of school staff, list your school's consequences for engaging in bullying behaviors. **Note:** If the language of the school's "official" list of consequences seems too difficult for the children in your class, be ready to explain and/or re-word the consequences for them so that they understand them. Arrange to have the principal in attendance to present the core of the session. Consider using the Optional Activity. See to it that the No-Bullying logo poster is displayed prominently in the meeting space.

Background for the Teacher

Even the youngest of children can understand the concept of consequences. Unfortunately, many children have experienced how consequences are not fairly applied. They need powerful reassurance that your school has no tolerance whatsoever for bullying and that your school will impose swift and strict consequences when it does occur. *Trust* is what is at stake here. The children need to trust that responsible and caring adults will intervene in bullying behavior and keep them safe.

Session Plan

Beginning the Session

Gather the children in a circle. Include the school principal in the circle, telling the children that he or she will be a visitor to their class today. Draw attention to the copy of the No-Bullying logo poster. Ask the children to explain its purpose. Afterward, go on to invite the children to recall the difference between tattling and telling. Ask:

- What gets someone *into* trouble, tattling or telling? (tattling)

- What gets someone *out of* trouble, tattling or telling? (telling)

Take time to correct any misunderstandings.

Leading the Session

1. Write the word "Consequences" on the board or newsprint. Ask if anyone knows what the word means. Record responses on the board or newsprint.

2. Draw on the children's ideas to help them devise a definition of consequences. Probably the easiest method is to help them recognize that once we say or do something, a consequence is *what might happen next*. Use the following questions as examples:

- If you put your hand in very hot water, what might happen next?
- If you win a race, what might happen next?
- If you eat too much at supper, what might happen next?
- If you bully someone at school, what might happen next?
- If you don't do your homework, what might happen next?

Go on to tell the children that their principal will talk to them about the consequences—about what will happen next—to people who bully others in their school.

3. The school principal will now address the children about your school's no-tolerance rule about bullying and about the consequences for engaging in bullying behavior. Make sure the principal has access to the poster of consequences you prepared prior to the session. The principal should also take time to reassure the children that school staff will support and protect victims of bullying.

4. When the principal completes his or her presentation, ask the children where they'd like to display the consequences in their classroom. Help the children post the list.

5. Briefly go through the list, letting the children know that you—and all the other adults in the school—agree with the consequences, promise to be supportive to students who tell about bullying and want to end it in their school, and pledge to protect all victims of bullying.

Concluding the Session

Invite the principal to join with the children in forming a circle around you. Direct them to place their arms around one another's shoulders. Set the copy of the No-Bullying logo poster on the floor in the center of the circle. Join the circle yourself. Then lead the children in singing "No More Bullies":

No More Bullies Song

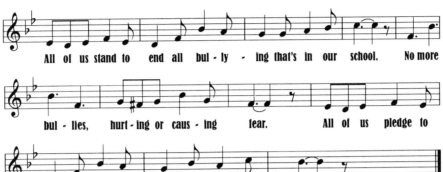

Ask the children and principal to show that they "stand together" and support one another in ending bullying in their school by taking six small steps forward, tightening the circle.

If you wish, conclude with handshakes or high-fives all around. Thank the children for all their good work and their willingness to end bullying in their school.

Optional Activity

Help the children remember the "Bullying Consequences" by making and giving each child a copy the consequences on index cards or easy-to-carry sheets that they can keep with them.

Teaching Masters

1. No-Bullying Logo Poster
2. No-Bullying Logos
3. What's Happening?
4. Bullying Denny
5. Feelings List
6. A Plan for Denny
7. Tattling or Telling?
8. Bullying Behavior Chart
9. No More Bullies Song

Teaching Master 2—No-Bullying Logos

WHAT'S HAPPENING?

1. I get bullied at school by being pushed, kicked, or hit.
   ☐ Never ☐ Once in awhile ☐ A lot ☐ Every day

2. I get bullied at school by name-calling, put downs, teasing, or being left out.
   ☐ Never ☐ Once in awhile ☐ A lot ☐ Every day

3. I bully others at school.
   ☐ Never ☐ Once in awhile ☐ A lot ☐ Every day

4. I think that most of the bullying that happens at our school happens
   ☐ in classrooms   ☐ in the bathrooms
   ☐ in hallways   ☐ in the cafeteria
   ☐ on the playground ☐ on the school bus

5. I get bullied on my way to and from school.
   ☐ Never ☐ Once in awhile ☐ A lot ☐ Every day

6. When I'm in school, I worry about being bullied.
   ☐ Never ☐ Once in awhile ☐ A lot ☐ Every day

7. If someone bullies me, I usually
   ☐ Tell the bully to stop   ☐ Tell another student
   ☐ Don't do anything   ☐ Tell an adult at school
   ☐ Tell my parents   ☐ I don't get bullied

8. If I see someone else getting bullied, I usually
   ☐ Help the victim   ☐ Join in the bullying
   ☐ Tell an adult at school ☐ Tell another student
   ☐ Tell my parents   ☐ Don't do anything

9. To help me feel safe at our school, I think adults should
   ☐ Make rules about bullying
   ☐ Enforce rules about bullying
   ☐ Teach more lessons about how to get along better
   ☐ Have better supervision of:
      ☐ school bus   ☐ bathrooms
      ☐ school grounds   ☐ hallways
      ☐ cafeteria   ☐ classrooms

Teaching Master 4—Bullying Denny

Bullying Denny

1st Student: You're such a nerd, Denny.
You're shoes are too shiny.

2nd Student: You're such a pain, Denny.
Your voice is so whiny.

3rd Student: You're such a klutz, Denny.
You can't ride a two-wheeler.

4th Student: You're such a dweeb, Denny.
You're also a squealer.

1st Student: I'm gonna get you right after lunch.
And when I get you, you'll get a punch.

2nd Student: I'm gonna poke you one, right in the eye.
And laugh in your face when you start to cry.

3rd Student: I might make you crawl, or better yet, dance.
'Cause if you don't, I'll pull down your pants.

4th Student: Maybe I'll kick you hard in the tush,
Or knock you or push you right into a bush.

All: Do you know who likes you? No one, that's who.
That's nobody, Denny. No one likes you!

Feelings List

afraid	disappointed	hopeful	powerful/less
aggressive	discouraged	hopeless	proud
amused	enthusiastic	hurt	rejected
angry	envious	inspired	relieved
anxious	excited	insecure	sad
appreciated	frightened	jealous	safe
bitter	frustrated	joyful	tense
bored	furious	lonely	unloved
concerned	glad	loved	wanted
confused	guilty	miserable	worthless
contented	happy	nervous	worthwhile

Teaching Master 6—A Plan for Denny

A Plan for Denny

Step 1: **Name the Problem.**

Denny's Problem: He is being bullied at school.

Step 2: **Know the Feelings.**

Circle all the words that tell how Denny feels.

happy	sad	proud	sick	angry
lonely	afraid	jealous	hurt	unloved

Step 3: **Ask for Help.**

Circle the names of people Denny could ask for help.

teacher	janitor	big kid	friend	principal

other:_____

Step 4: **Help Yourself**

Put an *X* by what you think is the best thing for Denny to do to help himself.

☐ get a stick to hit the bullies.   ☐ stay away from school.

☐ try to find some new friends.

☐ believe that adults can and will help.

☐ other:_____

Tattling or Telling?

Missy

Missy was waiting in line in the lunchroom. Allie was behind her in the line. As the line moved forward, Allie tripped on her shoelace and bumped into Missy. Missy slipped on some chocolate milk that someone had spilled on the floor and landed "kerplunk!" on her bottom. Missy was embarrassed. She pointed her finger at Allie and yelled at Ms. Post, the lunchroom aide, "That girl pushed me down!" Allie was sent to the principal's office.

Was Missy tattling or telling?   ❏ Tattling   ❏ Telling

Luiz

Every day Luiz went out to the play on the swings during recess. Every day Luiz saw and heard this big girl call a smaller boy in his class names. Whenever the big girl came around, the boy would leave or try to get out of the way. Even then, the girl would follow him and call him names. Luiz decided to talk to his teacher about what the big girl was doing.

Would Luiz be tattling or telling?   ❏ Tattling   ❏ Telling

Shanna

Mr. Thompson, the janitor, walked by the broom closet. Suddenly, he stopped. He could hear a noise coming from inside. Slowly, he opened the door. Someone was in there crying. Mr. Thompson switched on the light and saw Shanna hiding in the corner. Tears were running down her face. "What's the matter? Why are you crying and hiding in here?" Mr. Thompson asked. Shanna was embarrassed and afraid. She was embarrassed that Mr. Thompson found her hiding in the closet. She was afraid to say that her classmate, Leon, had chased her and threatened to hit her. Mr. Thompson knelt down next to Shanna and said, "Did someone hurt you? Did someone try to hurt you." Shanna started crying again. "Leon," she sobbed. "It was Leon."

Was Shanna tattling or telling?   ❏ **Tattling**   ❏ **Telling**

Jamhal

Miss Hill, the second grade teacher, said to her class, "No talking!" and told them to work on their drawings. All the children worked quietly, but Jamhal saw Leeanne ask Teresa to borrow a crayon. Jamhal jumped to his feet and said, "Miss Hill! Miss Hill! Leeanne and Teresa were bad. They were talking when you said not to."

Was Jamhal tattling or telling?   ❏ **Tattling**   ❏ **Telling**

Bullying Behavior Chart

LEVELS	Physical — Harm to another's body or property		Emotional — Harm to another's self-esteem		Social — Harm to another's group acceptance	
	verbal	non-verbal	verbal	non-verbal	verbal	non-verbal
1	Taunting Expressing physical superiority	Making threatening gestures Defacing property Pushing/shoving Taking small items from others	Insulting remarks Calling names Teasing about possessions, clothes	Giving dirty looks Holding nose or other insulting gestures Saying someone has germs or is unclean	Gossiping Starting/spreading rumors Teasing publicly about clothes, looks, etc…	Passively not including in group Playing mean tricks
2	Threatening physical harm Blaming victim	Damaging property Stealing Initiating fights Scratching Tripping or causing a fall Assaulting	Insulting family Harassing with phone calls Insulting intelligence, athletic ability, etc…	Defacing school work Falsifying school work Defacing personal property, clothing, etc…	Insulting race, gender Increasing gossip/rumors Undermining other relationships	Making someone look foolish Excluding from the group
3	Making repeated and/or graphic threats Practicing extortion Making threats to secure silence: "If you tell, I will…"	Destroying property Setting fires Biting Physical cruelty Making repeated, violent threats Assaulting with a weapon	Frightening with phone calls Challenging in public	Ostracizing Destroying personal property or clothing	Threatening total group exclusion	Arranging public humiliation Total group rejection/ostracizing

Bullying involves exploitation of a less powerful person. There must be an unfair advantage being exerted. Bully/victim conflict is best understood as a dynamic relationship. Whether or not a behavior is bullying depends on its effect upon the victim. This chart was designed to assist with the identification of bullying behavior in situations where an unfair advantage exists. The seriousness for all levels of behavior should be evaluated based on the harm to the victim and the frequency of the occurrences.

Teaching Master 9—No More Bullies Song

No More Bullies Song

No more bul - lies! That is our gol - den rule.

All of us stand to end all bul - ly - ing that's in our school. No more

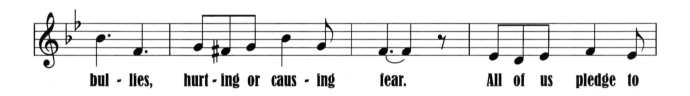
bul - lies, hurt - ing or caus - ing fear. All of us pledge to

work un - til there's no more bul - lies here.

Additional Resources

The following materials are available from the Johnson Institute. Call us at 800-231-5165 for ordering information, current prices, or a complete listing of Johnson Institute resources.

No-Bullying Program Materials

Tee shirts with the No-Bullying logo displayed on the front, posters, stickers, and extra teaching manuals for your school may be ordered simply by calling the sales department at Johnson Institute.

Video Programs

An Attitude Adjustment for Ramie. 15 minutes. Order #V429

Anger: Handle It Before It Handles You. 15 minutes. Order #V450

Broken Toy. 30 minutes. Order #V462

Choices & Consequences. 33 minutes. Order #V400

Conflict: Think About It, Talk About It, Try to Work It Out. 15 minutes. Order #V451

Dealing with Anger: A Violence Prevention Program for African-American Youth. 52 minutes (males), 68 minutes (females). Order #V433 (for males); Order #V456 (for females)

Double Bind. 15 minutes. Order #V430

Good Intentions, Bad Results. 30 minutes. Order #V440

It's Not Okay to Bully. 15 minutes. Order #5883JH

Peer Mediation: Conflict Resolution in Schools. 28 minutes. Order #V458Kit

Respect & Protect: A Solution to Stopping Violence in Schools and Communities. 28 minutes. Order #V460

Tulip Doesn't Feel Safe. 12 minutes. Order #V438

Publications

Bosch, Carl W. *Bully on the Bus.* Order #P413

Boyd, Lizi. *Bailey the Big Bully.* Order #P422

Carlson, Nancy. *Loudmouth George and the Sixth Grade Bully.* Order #P414

Crary, Elizabeth. *I Can't Wait.* Order #P431

———. *I'm Furious.* Order #P506

———. *I'm Mad.* Order #P509

———. *I Want It.* Order #P427

———. *My Name Is Not Dummy.* Order #P429

Cummings, Carol. *I'm Always in Trouble.* Order #P418

———. *Sticks and Stones.* Order #P420

———. *Tattlin' Madeline.* Order #P421

———. *Win, Win Day.* Order #P419

Davis, Diane. *Working with Children from Violent Homes: Ideas and Techniques.* Order #P244

DeMarco, John. *Peer Helping Skills Program for Training Peer Helpers and Peer Tutors.* Order #P320Kit

Estes, Eleanor. *The Hundred Dresses.* Order #P411

Fleming, Martin. *Conducting Support Groups for Students Affected by Chemical Dependence: A Guide for Educators and Other Professionals.* Order #P020

Freeman, Shelley MacKay. *From Peer Pressure to Peer Support: Alcohol and other Drug Prevention Through Group Process.* Order #P147-7-8 (for grades 7, 8); Order #P147-9-10 (for grades 9, 10); Order #P147-11-12 (for grades 11, 12)

Garbarino, James, et al. *Children in Danger.* Order #P330

Additional Resources

Goldstein, Arnold P., et al. *Aggression Replacement Training: A Comprehensive Intervention for Aggressive Youth.* Order #P329

Haven, Kendall. *Getting Along.* Order #P412

Johnsen, Karen. *The Trouble with Secrets.* Order #P425

Johnson Institute's No-Bullying Program for Grades K–Middle School. Order #546Kit

Julik, Edie. *Sailing Through the Storm to the Ocean of Peace.* Order #P437

Lawson, Ann. *Kids & Gangs: What Parents and Educators Need to Know.* Order #P322

Mills, Lauren A. *The Rag Coat.* Order #P417

Moe, Jerry, and Peter Ways, M.D. *Conducting Support Groups for Elementary Children K–6.* Order #P123

Olofsdotter, Marie. *Frej the Fearless.* Order #P438

Perry, Kate, and Charlotte Firmin. *Being Bullied.* Order #P416

Peterson, Julie, and Rebecca Janke. *Peacemaker® Program.* Order #P447

Potter-Effron, Ron. *How to Control Your Anger (Before It Controls You): A Guide for Teenagers.* Order #P277

Remboldt, Carole. *Solving Violence Problems in Your School: Why a Systematic Approach Is Necessary.* Order #P336

———. *Violence in Schools: The Enabling Factor.* Order #P337

Remboldt, Carole, and Richard Zimman. *Respect & Protect®: A Practical Step-By-Step Violence Prevention and Intervention Program for Schools and Communities.* Order #P404

Sanders, Mark. *Preventing Gang Violence in Your School.* Order #P403

Saunders, Carol Silverman. *Safe at School: Awareness and Action for Parents of Kids in Grades K–12.* Order #P340

Schaefer, Dick. *Choices & Consequences: What to Do When a Teenager Uses Alcohol/Drugs.* Order #P096

Schmidt, Teresa. *Anger Management and Violence Prevention: A Group Activities Manual for Middle and High School Students.* Order #P278

———. *Changing Families: A Group Activities Manual for Middle and High School Students.* Order #P317

———. *Daniel the Dinosaur Learns to Stand Tall Against Bullies. A Group Activities Manual to Teach K–6 Children How to Handle Other Children's Aggressive Behavior.* Order #P559.

———. *Trevor and Tiffany, the Tyrannosaurus Twins, Learn to Stop Bullying. A Group Activities Manual to Teach K–6 Children How to Replace Aggressive Behavior with Assertive Behavior.* Order #P558

Schmidt, Teresa, and Thelma Spencer. *Della the Dinosaur Talks About Violence and Anger Management.* Order #P161

Schott, Sue. *Everyone Can Be Your Friend.* Order #P435

Stine, Megan, and H. William Stine. *How I Survived 5th Grade.* Mahwah, NJ: Troll Associates, 1992. Order #P415

Vernon, Ann. *Thinking, Feeling, Behaving.* (for grades 1–6) Order #P250

Villaume, Philip G., and R. Michael Foley. *Teachers at Risk: Crisis in the Classroom.* Order #P401

Wilmes, David. *Parenting for Prevention: How to Raise a Child to Say No to Alcohol/Drugs.* Order #P071

———. *Parenting for Prevention: A Parent Education Curriculum—Raising a Child to Say No to Alcohol and Other Drugs.* Order #PO72T

ORDER FORM

BILL TO:

Name _____
Address _____
_____
City _____ State _____ Zip _____
ATTENTION: _____
Daytime Phone: ( ) _____
PURCHASE ORDER NO. _____

❏ Individual Order ❏ Group or Organization Order
If Ordering for a Group or Organization:
Group Name _____

SHIP TO: (if different from BILL TO)

Name _____
Address _____
_____
City _____ State _____ Zip _____
ATTENTION: _____
Daytime Phone: ( ) _____
TAX EXEMPT NO. _____

Please send me a free copy(ies) of Johnson Institute's:	❏ __ Publications and Films Catalog(s) ❏ __ Training Calendar(s) ❏ *Observer*, a quarterly newsletter

PLEASE SEND ME:

QTY.	ORDER NO.	TITLE	PRICE EACH	TOTAL COST

For film/video titles, please specify: ❏ 1/2" VHS   ❏ 3/4" U-Matic   ❏ 1/2" Beta   ❏ 16mm

---

SHIPPING AND HANDLING

Order Amount	U.S.	Outside U.S.
$0–25.00	$ 6.50	$8.00
$25.01–60.00	$ 8.50	$10.00
$60.01–130.00	$10.50	$13.50
$130.01–200.00	$13.25	$19.50
$200.01–300.00	$16.00	$24.00
$300.01–over	8%	14%

Please add $8.00 ($10.50 Canada) for any videotapes ordered.

OFFICE USE ONLY
Order No. _____
Customer No. _____

QVS, Inc.

❏ Payment enclosed
❏ Bill me
❏ Bill my credit card:

❏ MasterCard
❏ VISA
❏ American Express
❏ Discover

Expiration Date: _____
Signature on card: _____

Total Order _____
(Orders under $75.00 must be prepaid)

6.5% Sales Tax _____
(Minnesota Residents Only)

Shipping and Handling _____
(See Chart)

TOTAL _____

Have you ordered from the Johnson Institute before? **Yes** ❏   **No** ❏
If yes, how?   **Mail** ❏   **Phone** ❏

JOHNSON INSTITUTE®

7205 Ohms Lane ❖ Minneapolis, Minnesota 55439-2159
(612) 831-1630 or toll-free: 1-800-231-5165